Building Generational Wealth with Real Estate

Transforming Dreams into Generational Assets

By

Nike Oyelakin

Building Generational Wealth With Real Estate

Meet Nike Oyelakin

Nike Oyelakin is a dynamic force in both the literary and real estate worlds, blending her passion for writing with her expertise in property investment. Residing in the vibrant city of Houston, Texas, Nike navigates the realms of entrepreneurship, real estate, and family life with finesse.

As a devoted wife and mother, Nike understands the importance of building a secure future for her family. Drawing from her personal experiences and professional journey, she penned the insightful book "Building Generational Wealth With Real Estate." In this empowering guide, Nike shares practical strategies, invaluable tips, and firsthand wisdom on how individuals can leverage real estate to create lasting financial prosperity for themselves and future generations.

Nike Oyelakin's mission is clear: to empower individuals to build wealth, create legacies, and unlock their full potential through the transformative power of real estate.

Building Generational Wealth With Real Estate

Copyright

All rights reserved. No part of this publication may be reproduced, distributed, or transmitted in any form or by any means, including photocopying, recording, or other electronic or mechanical methods, without the prior written permission of the publisher, except in the case of brief quotations embodied in critical reviews and certain other noncommercial uses permitted by copyright law. Copyright © Nike Oyelakin, 2024

DISCLAIMER

This book's contents are intended only for informative purposes and do not represent financial, legal, or investment advice. The author and publisher make no guarantees or warranties about the accuracy or completeness of the material contained, and they expressly disclaim any implied warranties of merchantability or suitability for a particular purpose. Readers should perform their due research and speak with experienced specialists before making any financial choices. The author and publisher are not accountable for any losses or damages resulting from the use of the information provided in this book.

Building Generational Wealth With Real Estate

TABLE OF CONTENTS

Introduction

Chapter 1:Understanding Real Estate Investment Strategy

    Exploring Various Real Estate Investment Strategies

    Rental Properties: Passive Income from Property Ownership

    Fix-and-Flip: Turning Properties for Quick Profit

    Commercial Real Estate: Investing in Office, Retail, and Industrial Spaces

    Real Estate Investment Trusts (REITs): Diversifying with Securities

Developing a Long-Term Investment Plan

    Define Your Financial Goals and Vision:

    Assessing Risk Tolerance: Finding Your Comfort Zone:

    Creating a Timeline for Generational Wealth: Short-Term and Long-Term Goals

    Bibliography

Chapter 2: Recognizing Optimal Investment Prospects

    Implementing Market Research: Instruments and Methods

    Emerging Trends in Real Estate: Staying Ahead of the Curve

    Spotting Undervalued Properties: The Art of Deal Finding

Navigating the Real Estate Market

Understanding Supply and Demand Dynamics
Economic Indicators: Reading the Signs
Bibliography

Chapter 3: **Building Your Real Estate Portfolio**
Residential Properties: Foundations of Stability
Commercial Ventures: Exploring Opportunities Beyond Homes
Mixed-Use Properties: Maximizing Versatility and Income Potential

Leveraging Financing Options
Traditional Mortgages: Understanding Conventional Financing
Hard Money Loans: Quick Capital for Fix-and-Flip Ventures
Private Lenders and Creative Financing: Thinking Outside the Bank
Bibliography

Chapter 4: **Managing Investment Risks**
Mitigating Market Volatility: Strategies for Stability
Tenant Turnover: Ensuring Steady Rental Income
Property Maintenance: Preserving Asset Value and Attracting Tenants

Optimizing Property Management
Improving Property Value: Strategies for Long-Term Appreciation
Reduce Vacancies: Keeping Properties Occupied and Profitable

Maximizing Rental Income: Improving Your Property Management Practices

Bibliography

Chapter 5: **Utilizing Tax Advantages**

Depreciation Deductions: Maximizing Tax Benefits

Capital Gains Tax Exemptions: Strategies for Wealth Preservation

Transferring wealth to future generations

Estate Planning Essentials: Keeping Your Legacy

Reducing Estate Taxes: Strategies for Smooth Transitions

Providing a Smooth Transition of Ownership

Bibliography

Chapter 6:Building Your Credit

Building a Strong Credit Foundation: Advice for Beginners

Qualifying for Favorable Financing Terms

Accessing Loans for Real Estate Investment

The Dos and Don'ts of Loan Application

Requirements for Securing Real Estate Loans: Meeting Lender Criteria

Bibliography

Chapter 7: **Long-Term Buy and Hold Investments**

Principles of Long-Term Buy and Hold Investing

Advantages of Long-Term Buy and Hold

  Investments
  Strategies for Long-Term Buy and Hold Investments
  Multigenerational Home Ownership
Real Estate Development and Legacy Projects
  Real Property Development
  Legacy Projects
REITs and real estate syndications
  Real estate investment trusts (REITs)
  Types of REITs
  Real Estate Syndication
  Final Thoughts
  Bibliography

Introduction

Welcome to "Building Generational Wealth with Real Estate," a complete guide meant to empower you to achieve financial success and protect your family's future through smart real estate buying. In this book, we will explore proven strategies, expert insights, and practical tips to help you build and maintain wealth across multiple generations using real estate as a strong wealth-building tool.

In today's rapidly changing economic environment, standard paths of wealth building, such as savings accounts, stocks, and bonds, may no longer provide the financial security and steadiness needed to thrive in the long run. As economic risks continue and market turbulence becomes the new norm, smart investors are looking to alternative asset classes, such as real estate, to balance their portfolios, protect against inflation, and create passive income.

Real estate has long been regarded as one of the most reliable and time-tested tools for wealth building, offering unique benefits and possibilities for owners of all backgrounds and experience levels.

Throughout the pages of this book, you will start on a changing trip that will empower you to:

Understand the Fundamentals of Real Estate Investing: We will begin by putting the groundwork for success, studying the core principles of real estate investing, including market research, property value, financing choices, and risk management.

Throughout this journey, you will be guided by industry experts, successful investors, and real estate pros who will share their knowledge, insights, and best practices for building family wealth with real estate. Whether you're thinking of financial freedom, planning for retirement, or wanting to leave a legacy for your children and grandkids, this book will provide you with the inspiration, guidance, and practical help you need to turn your dreams into reality.

Are you ready to start on a changing journey toward financial freedom and family wealth? Let's begin our trip together and discover the endless possibilities of real estate investment!

Chapter 1

Understanding Real Estate Investment Strategy

Real estate investment provides a myriad of alternatives for investors looking to build wealth over time. In this chapter, we'll look at four types of real estate investment strategies: rental properties, fix-and-flips, commercial real estate, and real estate investment trusts. Each strategy has its own set of rewards, risks, and considerations, tailored to particular investor preferences and financial objectives.

Exploring Various Real Estate Investment Strategies

Real estate investment methods can be broadly divided into two types: active and passive. Active strategies involve hands-on management and direct participation in property transactions, whereas passive techniques require less involvement and frequently rely on third-party management or investment vehicles. Let's look at the aggressive and passive tactics in depth:

Rental Properties: Passive Income from Property Ownership

Investing in rental properties entails buying residential or commercial properties and renting them out to tenants in exchange for rental revenue. Rental properties provide investors with a consistent supply of passive income, frequently serving as a dependable source of cash flow over time. Furthermore, rental properties might rise in value over time, resulting in possible capital gains when sold.

One of the primary benefits of investing in rental properties is the option to use other people's money for financing. Obtaining a mortgage loan to acquire a property allows investors to benefit from the property's appreciation and rental income while only investing a portion of the entire value upfront.

However, to ensure profitability and avoid risks such as vacancies, property damage, and tenant conflicts, rental property investors must carefully pick properties, screen tenants, and maintain the properties themselves.

Fix-and-Flip: Turning Properties for Quick Profit

Fix-and-flip investment entails purchasing distressed or undervalued properties, remodeling or enhancing them, and then reselling them for a profit within a short time frame. This method appeals to investors seeking rapid returns on their investment cash. Successful fix-and-flip investors can locate properties with renovation potential, accurately estimate renovation expenses, and carry out renovation projects efficiently.

While fix-and-flip investing can produce large returns in a short period, it also entails tremendous risk.

Commercial Real Estate: Investing in Office, Retail, and Industrial Spaces

Commercial real estate investing is buying facilities utilized for business reasons, such as office buildings, shopping malls, and industrial complexes. Commercial properties often have more rental income than residential properties, making them appealing to investors looking for larger returns. commercial leases frequently have longer periods and may include opportunities for rent escalation, giving investors both income security and growth potential.

Investing in commercial real estate necessitates thorough due diligence and market analysis to discover assets with high revenue potential and suitable market conditions. Location, tenant quality, lease terms, and property condition are all factors that can have a substantial impact on investment profitability. Furthermore, commercial real estate investments may have higher initial expenditures, longer lease cycles, and greater exposure to economic downturns than residential assets.

Real Estate Investment Trusts (REITs): Diversifying with Securities

Real Estate Investment Trusts (REITs) allow investors to invest in real estate via publicly traded securities. REITs own and run income-generating properties such as apartment buildings, shopping malls, and office complexes, and pay out a large percentage of their taxable revenue to shareholders in the form of dividends. REITs allow investors to gain exposure to diverse real estate portfolios without having to own or manage the properties directly.

One of the key benefits of investing in REITs is liquidity, as shares may be purchased and sold on stock exchanges just like any other publicly traded company. REITs provide diversification benefits by allowing investors to distribute their money across various property kinds, geographic locations, and market sectors. However, REIT investments are vulnerable to stock market volatility and may not offer the same tax benefits as direct real estate ownership.

Developing a Long-Term Investment Plan

A long-term investing strategy is critical for those who want to accumulate money over time while limiting risks and attaining their financial objectives. In this chapter, we will look at the essential components of developing a complete long-term investment strategy, such as setting financial objectives and vision, determining risk tolerance, and creating a roadmap for generational wealth.

Define Your Financial Goals and Vision:

The first stage in developing a long-term investing strategy is to identify your financial objectives and vision. This includes determining what you want to accomplish with your assets, such as paying your retirement, saving for your children's education, acquiring a house, or reaching financial independence. Clarifying your objectives allows you to adjust your investing plan to meet your long-term goals.

When creating your financial objectives, keep them clear, measurable, attainable, relevant, and time-bound (SMART). Instead of just expressing that you want to "build wealth," you may establish a goal of saving a particular amount of money by a given age or attaining a target net worth within a certain period. By defining specific and concrete objectives, you can monitor your progress and keep motivated to stay on track.

Assessing Risk Tolerance: Finding Your Comfort Zone:

Risk tolerance is the willingness and capacity to endure variations in the value of your assets. Understanding your risk tolerance is critical for creating an investing strategy that fits your comfort level and financial situation.

Investors with a higher risk tolerance may be ready to tolerate more volatility in exchange for the possibility of better returns, while those with a lower risk tolerance may emphasize capital preservation and income stability.

When measuring your risk tolerance, you should take into account your investing time horizon, financial objectives, income stability, investment expertise, and emotional disposition.

Investors with longer time horizons and solid financial conditions may be willing to take on more risk, while those with shorter time horizons or larger financial obligations may choose a more cautious strategy.

To determine your risk tolerance, evaluate how you might respond to certain market situations, such as big variations in portfolio value or extended periods of market downturn.

Consider your capacity to absorb financial losses while maintaining your long-term financial objectives and emotional well-being. Understanding your risk tolerance allows you to create a well-balanced investment strategy that meets your specific goals and preferences.

Creating a Timeline for Generational Wealth: Short-Term and Long-Term Goals

Creating a timetable for generational wealth entails combining short-term and long-term financial objectives to develop a complete investment plan that spans numerous generations.

While short-term objectives may include milestones like saving for a down payment on a house or supporting a child's education, long-term goals are usually focused on retirement planning, estate preservation, and asset transfer.

When creating your generational wealth timeline, examine the time horizon for each of your financial objectives and prioritize them appropriately. Short-term objectives may need more conservative investing strategies centered on capital preservation and liquidity, while long-term goals may afford to take on greater risk in the quest for better returns.

Creating a long-term investment strategy entails setting clear financial goals and vision, analyzing your risk tolerance, and developing a schedule for generational wealth that balances short-term and long-term goals.

Bibliography

Smith, Gary W. "Real Estate Investing for Dummies." John Wiley & Sons, 2020.

Gallinelli, Frank. "What Every Real Estate Investor Needs to Know AboutCash Flow... And 36 Other Key Financial Measures." McGraw-Hill Education, 2015.

Linneman, Peter. "Real Estate Finance and Investments." McGraw-Hill Education, 2019.

Kiyosaki, Robert T. "Rich Dad's Guide to Investing: What the Rich Invest in, That the Poor and the Middle Class Do Not!" Plata Publishing, 2017.

Building Generational Wealth With Real Estate

Building Generational Wealth With Real Estate

Chapter 2

Recognizing Optimal Investment Prospects

Real estate investment opportunities that are profitable to acquire must be identified through a combination of market research, trend analysis, and the ability to identify undervalued properties.

This exhaustive guide aims to examine the methodologies and techniques involved in conducting market research, identifying lucrative investment opportunities, and maintaining an edge over emergent trends through deal finding.

Implementing Market Research: Instruments and Methods

Conducting market research is critical for achieving success in real estate investing as it offers indispensable knowledge regarding the intricacies of local markets, trends in supply and demand, and property valuations. The subsequent items and methods are fundamental to undertaking exhaustive market research:

Online databases and real estate websites, including Zillow, Realtor.com, and Redfin, provide users with access to extensive collections of property listings, historical sales data, and market trends. These platforms provide sophisticated search filters, interactive maps, and analytical tools that aid investors in the identification of prospective investment prospects and the real-time monitoring of market activity.

Local MLS (Multiple Listing Service): A licensed real estate agent or broker can grant you access to the local MLS database, which provides you with a more extensive selection of property listings and comprehensive property information.

Government and Census Data: Access publicly available data from government agencies, such as the U.S. Census Bureau and Bureau of Labor Statistics, to analyze demographic trends, population growth, employment rates, and economic indicators in target markets.

Local Networking and Industry Contacts: Build relationships with local real estate professionals, including agents, underwriters, appraisers, and property managers, to acquire insider knowledge and access off-market bargains. Networking with industry contacts can provide valuable insights into market trends, property availability, and investment opportunities that may not be publicly listed.

Property Investment Software and Analytics: Utilize specialized software and analytics tools designed for real estate investors to expedite property analysis, financial modeling, and investment decision-making. These tools offer features such as cash flow projections, investment performance metrics, and risk assessment tools to help investors evaluate potential investment opportunities and optimize portfolio performance.

Emerging Trends in Real Estate: Staying Ahead of the Curve

Staying aware of emergent trends is crucial for identifying profitable investment opportunities and capitalizing on market shifts before they become mainstream. Here are some significant emerging trends in real estate to watch out for:

Technology Integration: Embrace technology-driven solutions such as virtual reality excursions, online property management platforms, and smart home automation to enhance the tenant experience, improve operational efficiency, and differentiate your properties in the market.

Sustainable and Green Building Practices: Emphasize sustainability and environmental responsibility by investing in energy-efficient buildings, green infrastructure, and eco-friendly amenities to attract environmentally conscious tenants and reduce operating costs over the long term.

Urban Revitalization and Redevelopment: Explore opportunities in urban areas undergoing revitalization and redevelopment, such as downtown districts, historic neighborhoods, and transit-oriented developments, to capitalize on the demand for mixed-use properties, walkable communities, and urban lifestyle amenities.

Alternative Real Estate Asset Classes: Diversify your investment portfolio by investigating alternative real estate asset classes, such as student housing, senior living facilities, co-working spaces, and data centers, to delve into niche markets with strong demand drivers and growth potential.

Short-Term Rental and Vacation Properties: Take advantage of the expanding popularity of short-term rental platforms such as Airbnb and VRBO by investing in vacation properties, second residences, and rental units in tourist destinations, urban centers, and desirable vacation destinations.

Spotting Undervalued Properties: The Art of Deal Finding

Spotting undervalued properties is an essential skill for real estate investors seeking to uncover concealed jewels and capitalize on opportunities for value appreciation and profitability. Here are some strategies and techniques for mastering the craft of deal finding:

Distressed Properties and Foreclosures: Target distressed properties such as foreclosures, bank-owned residences, short sales, and properties in pre-foreclosure or distressed situations. These properties often sell below market value and present opportunities for renovation, rehabilitation, and value-added enhancements to increase their resale value.

Off-Market bargains and Pocket Listings: Network with real estate agents, wholesalers, property owners, and industry professionals to uncover off-market bargains and pocket listings not publicly listed on MLS or online platforms. Off-market agreements offer less competition and greater flexibility for negotiating favorable terms and prices.

Value-Add Opportunities: Look for properties with potential for value-add opportunities, such as cosmetic renovations, functional improvements, and repositioning strategies to enhance their appeal and marketability. Value-added investments enable investors to increase property value and rental income, resulting in higher returns on investment.

Market Mispricing and Inefficiencies: Identify market mispricing and inefficiencies by analyzing comparable sales, rental comps, and property valuation metrics to pinpoint properties priced below their intrinsic value or potential market value. By undertaking comprehensive due diligence and comparative analysis, investors can identify undervalued properties with strong upside potential.

Creative Financing and Negotiation: Explore creative financing options such as seller financing, lease options, seller concessions, and seller carryback mortgages to structure win-win agreements and negotiate favorable terms with motivated sellers. Creative financing strategies can help investors surmount financing challenges, reduce upfront costs, and increase investment flexibility.

Identifying profitable investment opportunities in real estate requires a multifaceted approach that incorporates market research, trend analysis, and deal-finding skills. By conducting comprehensive market research, remaining abreast of emerging trends, and mastering the art of deal finding, investors can uncover lucrative investment opportunities, capitalize on market inefficiencies, and achieve long-term success in real estate investing.

Navigating the Real Estate Market

Navigating the real estate market requires a thorough comprehension of supply and demand dynamics and the ability to interpret economic indicators that influence property values and market trends. In this exhaustive guide, we will examine these essential aspects of traversing the real estate market and provide insights into how investors can make informed decisions in this dynamic and ever-changing environment.

Understanding Supply and Demand Dynamics

Supply and demand dynamics play a fundamental role in defining the real estate market, and influencing property prices, rental rates, and investment opportunities. Let's delve into the main components of supply and demand dynamics in the real estate market:

Supply Factors: The supply side of the real estate market refers to the availability of properties for sale or rent within a given market. Supply factors include new construction activity, inventory levels, housing stock, and property development trends. High levels of new construction and increased housing supply can lead to downward pressure on prices and rental rates, while limited inventory and supply shortages can drive prices upward.

Demand Factors: The demand side of the real estate market represents the desire and ability of purchasers and tenants to purchase or rent properties. Demand factors comprise demographic trends, population growth, employment levels, consumer confidence, and affordability. Strong demand from purchasers and tenants, fuelled by favorable economic conditions and demographic shifts, can stimulate competition for properties and drive prices higher.

Market Equilibrium: The interplay between supply and demand ultimately determines market equilibrium, where the quantity of properties supplied equals the quantity demanded at a particular price point. In a balanced market, supply and demand are relatively in harmony, resulting in stable property prices and moderate levels of transaction activity. However, imbalances between supply and demand can lead to market fluctuations, peaks, or crashes.

Regional Variations: It's essential to recognize that supply and demand dynamics fluctuate across various geographic regions, communities, and property classifications. Local market conditions, economic trends, demographic shifts, and regulatory factors can influence supply and demand dynamics, creating opportunities and challenges for investors in specific markets.

Economic Indicators: Reading the Signs

Economic indicators provide valuable insights into the health and trajectory of the economy, influencing consumer behavior, investor sentiment, and real estate market trends. Here are some crucial economic indicators to consider when navigating the real estate market:

Gross Domestic Product (GDP): GDP measures the total value of products and services produced within a country's borders and functions as a broad indicator of economic activity and growth. A developing economy typically translates into increased consumer expenditure, business investment, and demand for real estate, propelling property values higher.

Employment and Unemployment Rates: Employment and unemployment rates reflect the labor market's health and affect individuals' ability to afford housing expenses, make mortgage payments, and qualify for home loans.

Low unemployment rates and stable job growth can bolster housing demand and support property values, while rising unemployment may contribute to decreased demand and weaker market conditions.

Interest Rates: Interest rates, set by central banks, influence financing costs, mortgage rates, and affordability for homebuyers. Lower interest rates stimulate housing demand by making mortgages more affordable, while higher interest rates can diminish demand and affordability, slowing down the real estate market's tempo and influencing property prices.

Inflation Rate: Inflation measures the rate of increase in the prices of products and services over time and affects consumers' purchasing power and the cost of living.

Moderate inflation can support real estate investment by preserving property values and rental income, while high inflation may erode purchasing power and diminish real returns on investment.

Housing Market Indicators: Specific indicators such as home sales, housing starts, building permits, and foreclosure rates provide insights into the health and activity of the housing market.

Rising home sales, increased construction activity, and declining foreclosure rates signal a robust housing market, while declining sales, stagnant construction, and rising foreclosures may indicate market challenges or downturns.

Monitoring economic indicators and comprehending their implications for the real estate market, investors can anticipate market trends, assess investment opportunities, and adjust their strategies accordingly to navigate the complexities of the real estate market effectively.

Navigating the real estate market requires a nuanced comprehension of supply and demand dynamics, as well as the ability to discern economic indicators that influence market trends and property values. By analyzing market fundamentals, monitoring economic indicators, and staying informed about local market conditions, investors can make informed decisions, mitigate risks, and capitalize on opportunities in the dynamic and ever-evolving real estate market.

Bibliography

Eldred, Gary W. "Investing in Real Estate." John Wiley & Sons, 2021.

Gray, Eric Tyson, and Robert S. "Real Estate Investing for Dummies." John Wiley & Sons, 2015.

Reilly, Frank K., and David M. "Real Estate Principles: A Value Approach."McGraw-Hill Education, 2019.

Ling, David C., and Wayne R. Archer. "Real Estate Principles: A Value Approach." McGraw-Hill Education, 2021.

Building Generational Wealth With Real Estate

Chapter 3

Building Your Real Estate Portfolio

Building a diversified real estate portfolio is essential for investors seeking to attain long-term wealth accumulation and financial security. In this guide, we will investigate three essential components of creating a robust real estate portfolio: Residential Properties, Commercial Ventures, and Mixed-Use Properties.

Each property type offers unique advantages and income potential, allowing investors to construct a well-rounded portfolio that balances stability, growth, and income generation.

Residential Properties: Foundations of Stability

Residential properties serve as the foundation of many real estate portfolios, offering stability, consistent cash flow, and long-term appreciation potential. Here's why residential properties are a cornerstone of successful real estate investing:

Steady Demand: Residential properties, including single-family homes, condominiums, and multi-family dwellings, pander to the fundamental human need for shelter, ensuring consistent demand regardless of economic conditions. This constant demand provides investors with a reliable source of rental income and occupancy stability, mitigating risks associated with vacancy and income fluctuations.

Diverse Tenant Base: Residential properties attract a diverse tenant base, including families, young professionals, students, and retirees, offering investors flexibility and versatility in tenant selection and rental strategies. By catering to various demographic segments and lifestyle preferences, investors can minimize tenant attrition, maximize rental income, and maintain occupancy levels even in competitive rental markets.

Appreciation Potential: Residential properties have historically demonstrated consistent appreciation over the long term, driven by factors such as population growth, urbanization, and housing market dynamics. While appreciation rates may vary by location and market conditions, residential properties generally provide investors with the opportunity to develop equity and wealth through property appreciation over time.

Accessibility and Affordability: Residential properties are accessible to a wide spectrum of investors, from first-time purchasers to seasoned investors, due to their relatively reduced barriers to entry compared to commercial real estate. Additionally, residential properties offer financing options such as conventional mortgages, FHA loans, and VA loans, making them more affordable and accessible to individual investors and small-scale proprietors.

Commercial Ventures: Exploring Opportunities Beyond Homes

Commercial real estate presents investors with opportunities to diversify their portfolios, capitalize on higher rental yields, and delve into niche markets with specialized property types.

Here's why commercial ventures are an attractive addition to a real estate portfolio:

Higher Rental Yields: Commercial properties, such as office buildings, retail centers, and industrial warehouses, typically command higher rental yields compared to residential properties, offering investors the potential for increased cash flow and higher returns on investment. Commercial leases often involve lengthier lease terms, annual rent escalations, and triple-net lease structures, providing investors with income stability and growth potential.

Professional Tenants and Corporate Clients: Commercial properties attract professional tenants, corporate clients, and business owners seeking quality office space, retail storefronts, and industrial facilities to conduct their operations. By leasing to established businesses with stable cash flow and creditworthiness, investors can minimize tenant turnover, reduce vacancy risk, and secure reliable rental income streams over the long term.

Market Diversification: Commercial real estate allows investors to diversify their portfolios across various property types, market sectors, and geographic regions, reducing concentration risk and exposure to specific market fluctuations.

Value-Add Opportunities: Commercial properties offer value-add opportunities for investors to enhance property value, optimize rental income, and improve property performance through strategic renovations, repositioning strategies, and lease negotiations. Value-added investments can generate higher returns on investment by unlocking unrealized value and maximizing property potential in competitive markets.

Investigating opportunities beyond residential properties and diversifying into commercial ventures, investors can access higher rental yields, professional tenants, and value-add opportunities, enhancing portfolio performance and growth potential.

Mixed-Use Properties: Maximizing Versatility and Income Potential

Mixed-use properties combine residential, commercial, and/or retail components within a single development, offering investors the opportunity to maximize versatility and income potential. Here's why mixed-use properties are a valuable addition to a real estate portfolio:

Synergistic Income Streams: Mixed-use properties generate multiple income streams from residential rentals, commercial leases, and retail tenants, providing investors with diversified revenue sources and income stability. By combining different property types within a single development, investors can create synergies and cross-market opportunities that enhance overall property value and tenant satisfaction.

Live-Work-Play Environments: Mixed-use developments create vibrant, live-work-play environments that appeal to contemporary urban residents desiring convenience, connectivity, and lifestyle amenities. By integrating residential units with commercial spaces, restaurants, shops, and recreational facilities, mixed-use properties attract diverse tenants and residents, nurturing community engagement and enhancing property appeal.

Adaptive Reuse and Urban Renewal: Mixed-use properties often involve adaptive reuse projects that repurpose existing structures or revitalization initiatives that transform underutilized areas into vibrant mixed-use developments. By leveraging existing infrastructure and repurposing obsolete properties, investors can release value, revitalize neighborhoods, and contribute
te to urban renewal efforts while generating attractive returns on investment.

Leveraging Financing Options

Financing is a crucial aspect of real estate investment, providing investors with the capital required to acquire properties, finance renovations, and develop their portfolios. In this guide, we will explore three essential financing options for real estate investors: Traditional Mortgages, Hard

Money Loans, and Private Lenders/Creative Financing. Each option offers unique advantages and considerations, allowing investors to customize their financing strategy to suit their investment objectives and circumstances.

Traditional Mortgages: Understanding Conventional Financing

Traditional mortgages, offered by banks and mortgage lenders, are the most prevalent form of financing for real estate investments. Here's how traditional mortgages function and their main features:

Down Payment and Loan Terms: Traditional mortgages typically require a down payment spanning from 3% to 20% of the property's purchase price, depending on the lender and loan program. The loan parameters vary but commonly include fixed-rate or adjustable-rate options with repayment periods of 15 to 30 years.

Qualification Requirements: To qualify for a traditional mortgage, applicants must satisfy certain eligibility criteria, including credit score, income verification, employment history, debt-to-income ratio, and property appraisal. Lenders assess the borrower's creditworthiness and financial stability to determine their ability to repay the loan.

Interest Rates and Closing Costs: Traditional mortgages offer competitive interest rates based on prevailing market rates and the borrower's credit profile. Additionally, applicants are responsible for paying closing costs, including loan origination fees, appraisal fees, title insurance, and escrow charges, which can vary depending on the lender and location.

Loan-to-Value (LTV) Ratio: Lenders calculate the loan-to-value ratio, which represents the percentage of the property's appraised value or purchase price that the loan covers. Lower LTV ratios indicate less risk for lenders and may result in more favorable loan terms for borrowers.

While traditional mortgages offer competitive rates and favorable terms, they require applicants to satisfy strict qualification requirements and provide a down payment, making them less accessible for some investors.

Hard Money Loans: Quick Capital for Fix-and-Flip Ventures

Hard money loans are short-term, asset-based loans provided by private lenders or investor organizations, offering fast access to capital for fix-and-flip ventures. Here's how hard money loans work and their main features:

Flexible Qualification Criteria: Unlike traditional mortgages, hard money lenders focus primarily on the property's value and potential profitability rather than the borrower's creditworthiness or income. As a result, hard money loans are accessible to investors with less-than-perfect credit or limited income documentation.

brief-Term Duration: Hard money loans typically have brief repayment terms varying from six months to three years, making them suitable for fix-and-flip ventures where investors intend to purchase, renovate, and sell properties swiftly for a profit. The short-term nature of hard money loans enables investors to capitalize on time-sensitive opportunities and maximize returns on investment.

Higher Interest Rates and Fees: Hard money loans carry higher interest rates and fees compared to traditional mortgages, reflecting the increased risk for lenders and the expedited funding process. Interest rates for hard money loans can range from 8% to 15% or higher, and consumers may also incur origination fees, points, and closing costs.

Loan-to-Value (LTV) Ratio: Hard money lenders typically offer financing based on the property's after-repair value (ARV), which represents the anticipated value of the property after renovations are completed. Hard money loans may cover up to 90% of the ARV, allowing investors to finance both the purchase price and renovation costs.

Hard money loans are ideal for real estate investors undertaking fix-and-flip projects who require rapid access to capital and flexible qualification criteria. While hard money loans offer expedited funding and flexibility, they come with higher interest rates and fees, making them suitable for short-term initiatives with high-profit potential.

Private Lenders and Creative Financing: Thinking Outside the Bank

Private lenders and inventive financing strategies offer alternative funding solutions for real estate investors seeking flexible terms and customized financing options.

Here are some examples of private lenders and creative financing methods:

Private Lenders: Private lenders, including individuals, family members, acquaintances, or private investment organizations, offer financing outside of traditional financial institutions. Private financiers may provide capital for various real estate projects, including fix-and-flip ventures, rental properties, or development projects, with flexible terms and negotiation opportunities.

vendor Financing: Seller financing entails the property vendor acting as the lender and financing a portion of the purchase price for the buyer. This arrangement enables purchasers to acquire properties with minimal down payment and closing costs, while vendors benefit from generating interest income and selling properties swiftly.

Subject-To Transactions: Subject-to-actions involve purchasing properties "subject to" the existing mortgage or financing terms, allowing investors to acquire properties without procuring new financing or qualifying for a loan. Subject-to transactions offer investors the flexibility to assume existing loans, avoid down payments, and leverage existing financing arrangements.

Lease Options and Rent-to-Own: Lease options and rent-to-own agreements provide tenants with the option to purchase the property at a predetermined price within a specified period, offering flexibility and affordability for aspiring homeowners. Investors can generate rental income while providing tenants with the opportunity to develop equity and eventually purchase the property.

Private lenders and inventive financing strategies offer investors alternative funding options beyond conventional mortgages and hard money loans, allowing for greater flexibility, negotiation opportunities, and customization to meet specific investment goals and circumstances.

Leveraging financing options is essential for real estate investors seeking to acquire properties, finance initiatives, and grow their portfolios.

By understanding the features and considerations of traditional mortgages, hard money loans, private lenders, and creative financing strategies, investors can tailor their financing approach to suit their investment objectives, risk tolerance, and financial circumstances, maximizing opportunities for success in the dynamic and competitive real estate market.

Bibliography

Geltner, David M., and Norman G. "Real Estate Finance and Investments:Risks and Opportunities." Lerner Press, 2017.

McLean, Scott, and Eldred, Gary W. "Investing in Real Estate." John Wiley & Sons, 2021.

Leveraging Financing Options:Brueggeman, William B., and Fisher, Jeffrey D. "Real Estate Finance &Investments." McGraw-Hill Education, 2020.

Reed, Scott. "Real Estate Finance: A Casebook." Cengage Learning, 2018.

Chapter 4

Managing Investment Risks

Managing investment risks is essential for real estate investors to secure their assets, preserve cash flow, and achieve long-term success in a dynamic and competitive market. In this exhaustive guide, we will explore three key areas of investment risk management:

Mitigating Market Volatility, Addressing Tenant Turnover, and Prioritizing Property Maintenance. By comprehending these risks and instituting proactive strategies, investors can minimize potential threats to their investment portfolio and optimize their returns.

Mitigating Market Volatility: Strategies for Stability

Market volatility, influenced by economic conditions, geopolitical events, and industry trends, can pose significant risks to real estate investments. Here are strategies to mitigate market volatility and maintain stability in your investment portfolio:

Diversification: Diversifying your real estate portfolio across various property types, geographic locations, and market segments can reduce exposure to specific market risks and mitigate against downturns in individual markets. By distributing investments across residential, commercial, and mixed-use properties, investors can mitigate the impact of market fluctuations on their overall portfolio performance.

Long-Term Investment Horizon: Adopting a long-term investment horizon allows investors to weather short-term market volatility and profit from the compounding effects of property appreciation and rental income over time. By focusing on the fundamental value of properties and retaining a patient approach to investment, investors can ride out market fluctuations and achieve sustainable growth in their portfolios.

Conservative Financing: Choosing conservative financing options with fixed interest rates, manageable debt levels, and adequate reserves can provide investors with financial stability and protection against rising interest rates or market downturns. Avoiding excessive leverage and maintaining liquidity can safeguard against potential cash flow disruptions and ensure financial flexibility during challenging economic conditions.

Active Risk Management: Implementing active risk management strategies, such as monitoring market trends, conducting regular property inspections, and staying informed about regulatory changes, allows investors to identify potential risks early and take proactive measures to mitigate them. By remaining vigilant and responsive to market dynamics, investors can adapt their investment strategy and defend their portfolios against unforeseen challenges.

Tenant Turnover: Ensuring Steady Rental Income

Tenant turnover, the process of tenants vacating properties and new tenants moving in, can disrupt cash flow and increase expenses for real estate investors. Here are strategies to address tenant attrition and ensure consistent rental income:

Tenant Screening and Selection: Conducting comprehensive tenant screening, including credit checks, income verification, and rental history analysis, helps identify reliable tenants who are likely to pay rent on time and maintain the property in good condition. By selecting high-quality tenants upfront, investors can reduce the risk of attrition and minimize the likelihood of rental income disruptions.

Long-Term Lease Agreements: Offering long-term lease agreements with stable tenants provides investors with income predictability and reduces the frequency of turnover. Long-term leases provide tenants with security and stability, incentivizing them to remain longer and renew their lease agreements, thereby minimizing vacancy periods and turnover-related expenses for investors.

Responsive Property Management: Providing responsive property management services, including timely maintenance, repairs, and tenant communication, enhances tenant satisfaction and retention. By addressing tenant concerns promptly and maintaining the property in good condition, investors can nurture positive tenant relationships, encourage lease renewals, and reduce turnover rates.

Tenant Incentives and Renewal Offers: Offering tenant incentives, such as rent discounts, lease renewal rebates, or enhancement incentives, can encourage existing tenants to renew their lease agreements and extend their occupancy. By rewarding loyal tenants and incentivizing lease extensions, investors can minimize turnover costs and maintain a stable rental income stream.

Property Maintenance: Preserving Asset Value and Attracting Tenants

Property maintenance plays a crucial role in preserving asset value, attracting quality tenants, and assuring tenant satisfaction. Here are strategies to prioritize property maintenance and enhance the value of your investment:

Preventive Maintenance: Implementing a proactive preventive maintenance program helps identify and resolve potential issues before they escalate into costly repairs or property damage. Regular inspections, routine maintenance duties, and timely restorations can prolong the lifespan of building systems and components, reduce maintenance expenses, and preserve the property's value over time.

Curb Appeal Enhancement: Enhancing curb appeal through landscaping, exterior enhancements, and cosmetic improvements can attract prospective tenants and create a positive first impression. Investing in exterior maintenance, such as lawn care, landscaping, painting, and signage, improves the property's visual appeal, enhances its marketability, and increases tenant satisfaction.

Responsive Repair Services: Providing responsive repair services and addressing tenant maintenance requests promptly demonstrates a commitment to tenant satisfaction and retention. By resolving maintenance issues promptly and preserving open communication with tenants, investors can nurture positive tenant relationships, minimize vacancy periods, and preserve rental income streams.

Upgrades and Renovations: Investing in upgrades and renovations, such as kitchen remodels, bathroom renovations, and interior improvements, can modernize the property, increase tenant demand, and justify higher rental rates. Strategic renovations that enhance functionality, aesthetics, and energy efficiency can attract quality tenants and maximize rental income potential, resulting in higher returns on investment.

managing investment risks in real estate requires a proactive approach to mitigate market volatility, resolve tenant attrition, and prioritize property maintenance.

Employing strategies to stabilize cash flow, minimize vacancy risk, and preserve asset value, investors can navigate market fluctuations and achieve sustainable growth in their real estate portfolio. By comprehending and addressing these key areas of investment risk management, investors can optimize their returns and create a resilient and profitable real estate portfolio over the long term.

Optimizing Property Management

Property management is an important part of real estate ownership since it has a direct influence on rental property performance and profitability. Effective property management includes increasing property value, reducing vacancies, and increasing rental revenue. In this detailed book, we will look at each of these areas in depth and present methods for improving property management procedures.

Improving Property Value: Strategies for Long-Term Appreciation

Improving property value is critical for maximizing return on investment and guaranteeing long-term growth. Here are some techniques to increase property value:

Regular Maintenance and Upkeep: Implementing a proactive maintenance program guarantees that the property is in excellent shape and retains its value over time. Regular inspections, periodic repairs, and preventive maintenance assist to avoid deterioration and treat problems before they become expensive.

Curb Appeal Enhancement: First impressions count, and improving the curb appeal of a house may have a major influence on its perceived worth. Investing in landscaping, external enhancements, and cosmetic changes may attract potential renters and raise rental prices. Simple improvements like new paint, updated lighting fixtures, and maintained landscaping may significantly improve the property's overall attractiveness.

Energy-efficient modifications not only save money on utilities but also raise the value of the property and attract environmentally conscientious renters. Consider investing in energy-efficient appliances, insulation, windows, and HVAC systems to boost the property's energy efficiency and save running costs over time.

Focus on modifications that increase property value and appeal to renters, such as kitchen remodels, bathroom renovations, flooring replacements, and smart home technology installs. Renovations that cater to tenant preferences and lifestyle trends might justify increased rental prices while attracting better renters.

Community facilities: Improving community facilities and common spaces may set the property apart from competition and attract residents looking for a better quality of life. Consider adding amenities like fitness centers, swimming pools, community areas, and pet-friendly facilities to improve tenant happiness and retention. Community facilities increase the overall appeal of the property and may justify higher rental fees.

Reduce Vacancies: Keeping Properties Occupied and Profitable

Minimizing vacancies is crucial for sustaining steady cash flow and increasing rental property profitability. Here are some techniques for reducing vacancies:

Effective Marketing and Advertising: Use a multi-channel marketing strategy to attract new renters and develop interest in the property. Use internet platforms, social media, rental listing websites, and local advertising to publicize open positions and attract a wide pool of candidates. To attract potential renters, highlight the property's distinctive characteristics, facilities, and location.

Tenant Retention Strategies: Prioritize tenant satisfaction and retention to decrease turnover and shorten vacancy times. Maintain open contact with renters, respond to their complaints quickly, and solve maintenance problems proactively to show your dedication to tenant happiness. Consider providing lease renewal incentives, such as rent reductions or upgrading possibilities, to entice current tenants to renew their leases and prolong their occupancy.

Competitive Rental Price: Conduct market research to identify competitive rental rates and verify that the property's price is in line with market trends and tenant demand. Pricing the property reasonably may help attract more quality applications and shorten the time it takes to fill vacancies. Consider giving incentives, such as move-in discounts or flexible lease terms, to attract new renters and speed up the leasing process.

Streamlined Application and Screening Process: Simplify the application and screening processes to improve tenant selection and reduce vacancy turnaround time. Use online rental applications, automated screening technologies, and electronic lease-signing platforms to speed up the leasing process and reduce administrative delays. Implement rigorous screening standards to assess potential renters' creditworthiness, rental history, and background checks to reduce risks and assure excellent tenants.

Responsive Property Management: Provide fast responses to tenant queries, maintenance requests, and complaints. Timely communication and effective problem-solving exhibit professionalism and dependability, which fosters strong tenant relationships and encourages loyalty. Property managers may improve tenant satisfaction and retention by maintaining high service and response standards, while also lowering turnover and vacancy rates.

By applying these tactics, investors may reduce vacancies, increase occupancy rates, and improve the profitability of their rental properties, resulting in long-term financial success and stability.

Maximizing Rental Income: Improving Your Property Management Practices

Maximizing rental revenue is critical for improving the financial performance of rental properties and increasing return on investments. Here are some ideas for optimizing property management procedures to increase rental income:

Market Rent Analysis: Conduct frequent market rent analysis to examine rental rates in the local market and verify that the property's price is competitive and in line with industry trends. Adjust rental prices regularly depending on market circumstances, demand-supply dynamics, and property upgrades to optimize rental revenue while preserving occupancy.

Value-Add Facilities and Services: Determine which facilities and services appeal to renters and justify higher rental fees. Consider providing extra services such as pet-friendly accommodations, parking, storage spaces, laundry services, or furnished apartments to increase the property's value proposition and fetch higher rates. Value-added facilities improve tenant happiness and retention while boosting rental revenue possibilities.

Incremental Rent Increases: Use incremental rent increases at lease renewal to capitalize on market appreciation and optimize rental revenue over time. Gradual rent increases, in line with inflation rates and market trends, enable owners to boost rental revenue while reducing tenant turnover and vacancy risk. Rent increases should be straightforwardly communicated to renters, with early notice provided to aid lease renewal talks.

charge Optimization: Examine and optimize charge structures such as application fees, late fees, pet fees, and parking fees to increase ancillary income and supplement rental revenue. Ensure that costs are competitive and in line with industry norms, while adhering to local rules and fair housing legislation.
Transparent fee transparency and equitable charge procedures improve tenant satisfaction and retention.

Expense Management: Efficiently manage operational expenditures to maximize cash flow and net rental revenue. Implement cost-cutting initiatives, negotiate vendor contracts, and look into energy-efficient alternatives to cut utility bills, maintenance charges, and property management fees. Review spending reports, budget estimates, and financial performance data regularly to find cost-saving options and increase profitability.

Improving property management methods includes increasing property value, reducing vacancies, and increasing rental revenue to optimize return on investment and achieve long-term profitability.

Applying proactive tactics and fine-tuning property management procedures, investors may improve the performance of their rental properties, attract excellent tenants, and gradually establish a robust and successful real estate portfolio.

Bibliography

Herring, F. "Investing in Real Estate." Routledge, 2020.

Rogan, R. "Managing Real Estate Portfolios: A European Perspective."Routledge, 2016.

Hwang, Brian J., and Hwang, H. "Property Management Accounting: ASurvival Guide for Non-Accountants." John Wiley & Sons, 2018.

Levy, Sidney. "Investment Performance Measurement: Evaluating and
Presenting Results." John Wiley & Sons, 2018.

Chapter 5

Utilizing Tax Advantages

Tax benefits are important in real estate investing because they allow investors to reduce their tax bills, maximize their gains, and protect their wealth. In this thorough tutorial, we will look at three main tax benefits for real estate investors: depreciation deductions, capital gains tax exemptions, and 1031 exchanges.

Understanding and using these tax advantages may assist investors in optimizing their investing plans and achieving long-term financial success.

Depreciation Deductions: Maximizing Tax Benefits

Depreciation is a tax deduction that helps real estate investors gradually recoup the cost of an income-producing property. Here's how depreciation deductions operate and how to maximize this tax benefit:

Understanding Depreciation: Depreciation is a non-cash expenditure that accounts for the progressive wear and tear, deterioration, or obsolescence of a property over its useful life. The

Internal Revenue Service (IRS) permits investors to depreciate the cost of residential and commercial properties over 27.5 and 39 years, respectively, utilizing the Modified Accelerated Cost Recovery System (MACRS) method.

Maximizing Depreciation Deductions: To maximize depreciation deductions, investors should effectively allocate expenses to depreciable assets, keep precise records of property modifications, and use accelerated depreciation techniques as needed. Proper depreciation planning may dramatically decrease taxable income, enhance cash flow, and improve the overall tax efficiency of real estate assets.

Depreciation Recapture: It is critical to understand depreciation recapture regulations, which force investors to recoup and pay taxes on depreciation deductions claimed when selling real estate. Depreciation recapture is taxed at a greater rate than capital gains, underlining the need for tax preparation and exit options in reducing tax liability upon property transfer.

Real estate investors who use depreciation deductions properly may lower taxable income, boost cash flow, and improve the overall tax efficiency of their investment portfolio.

Capital Gains Tax Exemptions: Strategies for Wealth Preservation

Capital gains tax exemptions enable real estate owners to deduct or delay taxes on capital gains obtained from the sale of investment properties. Here are techniques for increasing capital gains tax exemptions while protecting wealth:

The primary residence exclusion allows homeowners to exclude up to $250,000 ($500,000 for married couples filing jointly) in capital gains from the sale of their primary residence if they have owned and occupied the property as their principal residence for at least two of the previous five years.

1031 Like-Kind Exchanges: A 1031 exchange enables investors to delay capital gains taxes on the sale of investment properties by reinvesting the profits in comparable replacement properties.
A 1031 exchange allows investors to delay taxes forever and leverage their equity to buy bigger or higher-performing properties without incurring immediate tax repercussions.

Qualified Opportunity Zones (QOZs): Qualified Opportunity Zones are economically challenged locations where investors may delay or eliminate capital gains taxes by investing capital gains from the sale of valuable assets in qualified opportunity funds (QOFs).

Investing in QOFs and qualifying properties in Opportunity Zones allows investors to defer capital gains taxes until 2026 and potentially reduce or eliminate taxes on future appreciation, providing significant tax breaks for long-term wealth preservation and investment in underserved communities.

Estate Planning Strategies: Techniques such as gifting, trusts, and charity giving may assist real estate investors in transferring wealth to future generations while lowering estate and capital gains taxes. By properly structuring asset ownership and disposal, investors may protect their wealth, reduce tax costs, and guarantee a seamless succession of ownership to heirs or beneficiaries.

Transferring wealth to future generations

Real estate investors must consider passing money down to future generations as part of their estate planning. Effective estate planning includes safeguarding your legacy, lowering inheritance taxes, and guaranteeing a seamless transfer of ownership via family governance and succession planning. In this book, we will look at each of these components and provide techniques for effortlessly transferring money down to future generations.

Estate Planning Essentials: Keeping Your Legacy

Estate planning is the act of structuring and managing your assets so that your desires are carried out after your death or incapacity. Preserving your legacy entails defining your goals, safeguarding your assets, and providing for your heirs. Here are some estate planning basics for real estate investors:

Will: A will is a legal document that specifies how you want your possessions distributed and who should care for your young children. In your will, you may indicate how your real estate assets should be divided to your heirs, designate beneficiaries, and choose an executor to manage your estate.

Setting up trusts helps you to safeguard assets, avoid probate, and regulate the transfer of money over time. Revocable living trusts, irrevocable trusts, and testamentary trusts are three common forms of trusts used in estate planning.

Beneficiary Designations: Review and amend beneficiary designations on retirement accounts, life insurance policies, and other assets to verify they are consistent with your estate planning objectives. Designating beneficiaries directly on these accounts may avoid probate and allow for the prompt transfer of assets to heirs.

Reducing Estate Taxes: Strategies for Smooth Transitions

Estate taxes may dramatically reduce the value of an estate and the wealth handed down to heirs. Estate tax minimization requires strategic planning and the use of tax-saving methods to retain wealth. Here are some techniques to reduce estate taxes:

Lifetime Gifting: You may use the yearly gift tax exclusion and lifetime estate tax exemption to transmit assets to heirs tax-free throughout your lifetime. The yearly gift tax exclusion permits you to give up to a set amount ($15,000 per recipient in 2022) to people without paying gift taxes. Furthermore, the lifetime estate tax exemption ($12.06 million per person in 2022) permits you to transfer assets that exceed the yearly exclusion threshold without incurring estate tax.

Irrevocable Life Insurance Trust (ILIT): Create an irrevocable life insurance trust to store life insurance policies outside of your estate while protecting the death benefit from estate taxes. By transferring ownership of life insurance policies to an ILIT, you remove the profits from your taxable estate, allowing you to meet estate taxes and other expenditures without depleting your other assets.

Providing a Smooth Transition of Ownership

Family governance and succession planning are critical for ensuring a seamless transfer of ownership and administration of real estate assets to subsequent generations. Here are some important aspects for good succession planning:

Family meetings and communication: Encourage family members to communicate openly and transparently about estate planning objectives, asset transfer techniques, and future expectations. Regular family meetings allow for the discussion of difficult themes, the resolution of problems, and the alignment of goals, ensuring a cohesive approach to succession planning.

Identifying Successors and Roles: Look for family members who are interested, capable, and committed to taking over ownership and management of real estate holdings. Clarify the roles and responsibilities of each successor, including decision-making power, operational obligations, and long-term strategic planning.

Training and Development: Invest in future generations' education and training to equip them for leadership positions in real estate asset management. Provide education, coaching, and hands-on experience in property management, financial planning, and investment strategy to ensure that successors have the essential skills and expertise to succeed.

Bibliography

Meckler, H. "Tax Strategies for the Small Investor:A Comprehensive Guideto Tax Planning Techniques." John Wiley & Sons, 2019.

Wiedemer, David. "The Aftershock Investor: A Crash Course in Staying Afloat in a Sinking Economy." John Wiley & Sons, 2013.

Turcan, R. "Family Trusts: A Guide for Beneficiaries, Trustees, Trust Protectors, and Trust Creators." Atlantic Publishing Company, 2015.

Coombs, J. "Creating Family Wealth: Ethics, Responsibilities, and Legacy."
Business Expert Press, 2019.

Chapter 6

Building Your Credit

Building a good credit foundation is critical for real estate investors seeking to qualify for advantageous financing conditions, access investment possibilities, and achieve long-term financial success.

In this tutorial, we'll look at crucial tactics for building and keeping good credit, as well as how to qualify for attractive financing arrangements in real estate investing.

Building a Strong Credit Foundation: Advice for Beginners

For newcomers, establishing a good credit foundation entails creating a positive credit history and practicing prudent credit behaviors. Here are some suggestions to get started:

Obtain a Credit Card: Apply for a secured or student credit card to begin building a credit history. Secured credit cards demand a security deposit, making them available to those who have little or no credit history. To establish trustworthiness, use the credit card sensibly, making little purchases and paying off the debt in whole and on time each month.

Become an Authorized User: If you have a family member or acquaintance with a good credit history, ask them to add you as an authorized user to their credit card account. As an approved user, you may benefit from their existing credit history and favorable payment habits, which can help you develop credit faster.

Pay Bills on Time: Making timely payments on bills such as credit cards, student loans, and utility bills is critical for developing a solid credit history. Set up automated payments or reminders to make sure your bills are paid on time every month. Late payments may significantly lower your credit score and eligibility for future lending.

Limit Credit Applications: Avoid applying for several credit cards or loans in a short period, since each application causes a hard inquiry on your credit report, thereby lowering your credit score. Be careful when applying for new credit, and only seek credit accounts that you need.

By following these guidelines, novices may establish the foundations for a solid credit foundation and position themselves for future financial success in real estate investing.

Maintaining Healthy Credit: Best Practices for Long-term Success Once you've built credit, keeping good credit practices is critical for long-term success. Here are the greatest strategies for preserving good credit:

Keep Credit Card Balances Low: Keep credit card balances low in comparison to your credit limits, since excessive credit usage ratios might harm your credit score. To show appropriate credit management, restrict your credit card utilization to 30% of your available credit limit.

Avoid Closing Old Accounts: The length of your credit history is a crucial element in determining your credit score, so keep old credit card accounts open even if you no longer use them regularly. Keeping old accounts active will help boost the average age of your credit accounts and eventually enhance your credit score.

Diversify Your Credit Mix: Having a varied range of credit accounts, including credit cards, installment loans, and student loans, will help your credit score. However, only open new credit accounts if you can handle them properly and avoid overextending yourself financially.

Regularly Review Your Credit Report: Keep an eye on your credit report for any changes or abnormalities, such as unauthorized accounts or fraudulent activities. Report any suspicious activity to the credit bureaus immediately and take precautions to safeguard your identity and credit information.

Use Credit Responsibly: Avoid actions that might harm your credit score, such as maxing out credit cards, skipping payments, or defaulting on loans. Building a track record of prudent credit management shows lenders that you are a dependable borrower, which increases your chances of qualifying for favorable lending arrangements.

Qualifying for Favorable Financing Terms

To get access to investment possibilities and optimize earnings, real estate investors must first qualify for advantageous financing arrangements. Tips for qualifying for good loan terms:

Improve Credit Score: Work on raising your credit score by exercising good credit behaviors including paying bills on time, keeping credit card balances low, and having a diversified mix of credit accounts.

A higher credit score boosts your chances of qualifying for cheaper interest rates and more favorable loan arrangements.

Reduce Debt-to-Income Ratio: Lenders use their debt-to-income (DTI) ratio to determine their capacity to handle more debt responsibly. Reduce your DTI ratio by paying down current debts, boosting income, or lowering spending. A lower DTI ratio indicates financial stability and may increase your eligibility for loans.

Save for a Higher Down Payment: Making a higher down payment will increase your loan-to-value (LTV) ratio and minimize the amount of financing necessary, making you a more appealing borrower to lenders. Furthermore, a greater down payment may qualify you for cheaper interest rates and more favorable loan conditions.

Shop Around for Lenders: Don't accept the first financing offer you get—shop around and compare loan conditions from numerous lenders to obtain the best price. When examining financing choices, take into account interest rates, loan terms, closing expenses, and lender reputation.

Consider Government-Backed Lending Programs: For qualified applicants, government-backed lending programs like FHA loans, VA loans, or USDA loans may provide more lenient credit standards and lower down payments.

Accessing Loans for Real Estate Investment

Loans are an essential component of real estate investing, allowing investors to purchase properties, extend their portfolios, and capitalize on possibilities for development.

Navigating the loan application procedure, satisfying lender requirements, and positioning oneself for loan acceptance are all necessary aspects of obtaining funding for real estate investing. In this thorough tutorial, we will go over each of these components in depth, giving insights and tactics for effectively securing loans in the real estate market.

The Dos and Don'ts of Loan Application

The loan application procedure may be complicated and intimidating, particularly for first-time investors. Understanding the do's and don'ts may assist speed up the process and boost the chances of loan acceptance. Here are some important considerations:

Dos:

Prepare Financial Documentation: Gather any relevant financial documents, such as tax returns, bank statements, pay stubs, and asset statements, to present a complete picture of your financial condition. Preparing these papers ahead of time can speed up the application process and establish your trustworthiness to lenders.

Check your credit report. Get a copy of your credit report from all three main credit bureaus—Equifax, Experian, and TransUnion—and check it for accuracy.

Dispute any inaccuracies or inconsistencies on your credit report as soon as possible to ensure that it accurately represents your credit history and increases your chances of loan acceptance.

Enhance your Credit Score: Before applying for a loan, work to enhance your credit score by paying down current debts, settling any collections or judgments, and correcting any bad entries on your credit report. A higher credit score boosts your chances of qualifying for better loan conditions and interest rates.

Shop around for lenders: Compare interest rates, fees, and loan conditions from a variety of lenders, including banks, credit unions, mortgage brokers, and internet lenders. Shopping around helps you to get the greatest loan choice that fits your financial needs and preferences.

Consider receiving pre-approval for a loan before beginning your home hunt. Pre-approval gives you a clear picture of your borrowing capacity and enhances your offer when competing against other purchasers in a competitive market.

Don'ts:

Apply for Many Loans Simultaneously: Avoid applying for many loans at the same time since each one causes a hard inquiry on your credit report, which may temporarily damage your credit score. Instead, apply for loans selectively and target funding possibilities that you are serious about.

Overlook Loan Terms and Fees: Pay attention to loan conditions, such as interest rates, repayment schedules, prepayment penalties, and closing charges. Examine the loan estimate offered by lenders to comprehend the overall cost of borrowing and prevent surprises at closing.

Misrepresenting Financial Information: When submitting financial information to a lender, be honest and straightforward. Misrepresenting income, assets, or obligations may result in loan refusal or possibly legal action. Provide accurate and reliable evidence to support your loan application and foster confidence with lenders.

Ignore Debt-to-Income Ratio: When asking for a loan, lenders look at your debt-to-income (DTI) ratio to see if you can repay the loan. To increase your chances of loan acceptance, maintain your DTI ratio below the lender's maximum level.

Loan Conditions: Pay particular attention to the loan terms and criteria given by the lender, such as property appraisals, title searches, and insurance coverage. Fulfilling these requirements in a timely way is critical for ultimate loan approval and deal completion.

Requirements for Securing Real Estate Loans: Meeting Lender Criteria

Meeting lender requirements is critical for acquiring real estate loans and funding for investment properties. When evaluating loan applications, lenders consider a variety of characteristics, including creditworthiness, income stability, property value, and debt-to-income ratio. Here are the essential prerequisites for obtaining a real estate loan:

A good credit history is one of the main conditions for obtaining a real estate loan. Lenders use credit scores and credit records to measure borrowers' creditworthiness and chance of repaying the loan. Maintain a decent credit score by making regular payments, reducing debt, and avoiding unfavorable notes on your credit record.

Low Debt-to-Income Ratio: The debt-to-income (DTI) ratio compares your monthly debt payments to your gross monthly income. Lenders normally need a DTI ratio of 43% or less to qualify for a mortgage. Calculate your DTI ratio and take measures to decrease debt or boost income as needed to fulfill lender criteria.

Property Appraisal: Lenders demand a property appraisal to determine the worth of the property and guarantee that it will serve as appropriate collateral for the loan. Hire a skilled appraiser to do a complete evaluation
of the property and offer an accurate value.

Bibliography

Griffin, R. "Credit Repair Kit for Dummies." John Wiley & Sons, 2018.

Allayannis, G., and Brown, G. "Managing Credit Risk in Corporate BondPortfolios: A Practitioner's Guide." World Scientific Publishing Company, 2019.

Chiang, C., and Lee, A. "Real Estate Finance and Investment: Risks and Opportunities." World Scientific Publishing Company, 2021.

Arzac, E. "Financing International Real Estate." Springer, 2017.

.

Building Generational Wealth With Real Estate

Building Generational Wealth With Real Estate

Chapter 7

Long-Term Buy and Hold Investments

Long-term buy-and-hold investment is a real estate strategy in which investors acquire properties to keep them for a lengthy period, usually five years or more. This strategy focuses on creating passive income via rental properties, increasing equity through property appreciation, and taking advantage of tax breaks to optimize returns. In this thorough book, we will look at the ideas, rewards, and techniques for long-term real estate investment.

Principles of Long-Term Buy and Hold Investing

Long-term buy-and-hold investment requires patience and tenacity. Investors must be prepared to weather market changes, economic downturns, and property management difficulties while holding onto their assets for a lengthy period.

Cash Flow Generation: Long-term purchase and hold investment aims to generate cash flow. Investors want to produce steady rental revenue from their properties to meet mortgage payments, running costs, and passive income. Positive cash flow ensures financial security and enables investors to reinvest gains in new properties or retirement savings.

Equity Build-Up: As renters pay down their mortgage principal over time, the investor's ownership interest in the property grows. Long-term investors profit from the steady buildup of equity, which increases their net worth and offers financial stability. Equity building also allows investors to get extra funding for future ventures via cash-out refinancing or home equity loans.

Property Appreciation: Property appreciation is the growth in value of real estate assets over time. Long-term buy-and-hold investors profit from property appreciation, which may be driven by inflation, market demand, economic expansion, and property renovations. While property prices vary in the near term, real estate has traditionally appreciated over time, allowing investors to accumulate significant wealth.

Tax Advantages: Long-term buy-and-hold investors take advantage of a variety of tax breaks and incentives to enhance their investment profits. Depreciation deductions, capital gains tax exemptions, 1031 exchanges, and property and mortgage interest deductions are all examples of tax breaks. By enhancing tax efficiency, investors may reduce tax bills while increasing total investment returns.

Advantages of Long-Term Buy and Hold Investments

Long-term buy-and-hold investment offers investors with a steady stream of passive income from rental properties. Monthly rental payments from renters help to generate positive cash flow, which may augment other sources of income and give financial stability, especially in retirement.

Long-term buy-and-hold investment promotes wealth creation via equity growth and property appreciation. As renters pay off their mortgages and property prices rise over time, investors accumulate equity in their real estate assets, boosting their net worth and generating long-term prosperity.

Real estate may be used as a hedge against inflation since property prices and rental revenue tend to grow in response to inflationary pressures. Long-term investors benefit from real estate assets' capacity to maintain buying power and provide a consistent income stream that keeps up with inflation over time.

Portfolio diversity: Real estate provides diversity advantages to investors by serving as an alternative asset class with a low connection to typical equities and bonds. Including real estate in a diversified investment portfolio may lower total portfolio risk while increasing risk-adjusted returns, especially during times of market volatility.

Tax Efficiency: Long-term purchase and hold investment provides considerable tax benefits, such as depreciation deductions, capital gains tax exemptions, and 1031 Exchanges. By taking advantage of these tax breaks, investors may reduce tax bills, enhance cash flow, and maximize long-term investment returns.

Strategies for Long-Term Buy and Hold Investments

Location Selection: Look for homes in attractive areas with solid fundamentals like employment growth, population expansion, excellent schools, and amenities. Look for communities with low crime rates, significant rental demand, and potential for long-term growth.

Property Selection: Choose properties that match your investing objectives, risk tolerance, and budget. Consider the following factors: property type (single-family houses, multifamily properties, commercial real estate), condition, age, size, and rental potential. To find viable investment prospects, do rigorous due diligence such as property inspections, financial analysis, and market research.

finance plan: Create a finance plan that maximizes leverage while minimizing risk. Investigate financing alternatives such as conventional mortgages, FHA loans, VA loans, and portfolio loans to get advantageous terms and maximize profits. When examining financing choices, take into account interest rates, loan terms, down payment requirements, and cash flow estimates.

Property Management: Use excellent property management strategies to increase rental revenue, reduce vacancies, and maintain property value. Tenants should be thoroughly screened, lease terms enforced, and premises maintained regularly to guarantee tenant satisfaction and retention. Consider outsourcing property management responsibilities to professional management firms to simplify operations and maximize profits.

Long-Term Vision: Maintain a long-term investing view and avoid making rash choices based on short-term market volatility. Focus on purchasing high-quality properties, increasing equity, and reinvesting revenues for future development. Periodically examine your investment portfolio, analyze market circumstances, and change your approach to correspond with shifting goals and objectives.

Multigenerational Home Ownership

Multi-generational home ownership is the practice of numerous generations living together in a single household, either by choice or necessity. Economic, cultural, and demographic issues have all contributed to the rise in popularity of this arrangement.

Benefits of Multigenerational Home Ownership

Cost Savings: Multigenerational house ownership enables families to pool financial resources and share living costs, resulting in considerable cost savings. By sharing home expenditures such as mortgage payments, property taxes, utilities, and maintenance fees, each generation may lessen its financial load and achieve better affordability.

Shared duties: Living in a multigenerational home fosters teamwork and shared duties among family members. Each generation may bring their talents, resources, and knowledge to help the home and satisfy communal requirements. Families may improve their daily efficiency and balance by dividing domestic duties, caregiving responsibilities, and financial commitments.

Real Estate Development and Legacy Projects

Real estate development is the process of acquiring, developing, building, and managing assets to add value and earn profits for investors. Legacy projects, on the other hand, are long-term, visionary enterprises that leave an indelible mark on communities and future generations.

Real Property Development

Real estate development is a broad collection of operations aimed at converting raw land or existing buildings into valuable assets. Developers are responsible for recognizing opportunities, arranging money, acquiring permits, supervising construction, and selling properties to end users and investors. The real estate development process generally consists of the following stages:

Site Selection and Acquisition: Developers choose ideal development sites based on location, market demand, zoning rules, and accessibility. Once a site has been identified, developers negotiate purchase agreements and get the required permissions and entitlements to go forward with the project.

Planning and Design: Developers work with architects, engineers, and other specialists to develop a detailed project plan and design. This step involves envisioning the idea, creating architectural drawings, securing regulatory clearances, and completing construction plans.

Financing and Capitalization: Developers get financing and capital for their projects from a variety of sources, including bank loans, private equity, joint ventures, and crowdsourcing. They collaborate with lenders, investors, and financial consultants to develop financing plans that satisfy the project's capital requirements and investment goals.

Construction & Development: Once finance has been acquired, developers will manage the project's construction and development following the authorized designs and specifications. They supervise contractors, subcontractors, and

Marketing and Sales: Once construction is completed, developers promote and sell or lease the properties to end users or investors. They use sales and marketing methods to attract buyers or renters, negotiate contracts, and smooth real estate transactions.

Management and Operations: After the project is completed, developers may remain active in property management and operations, especially for commercial buildings. They manage leasing, tenant relations, maintenance, and continuous capital upgrades to increase the property's value and investment returns.

Successful real estate development requires a mix of market understanding, financial competence, project management abilities, and creative vision. Developers must overcome regulatory constraints, market factors, and construction hazards to complete projects and provide value for stakeholders.

Legacy Projects

Legacy projects are ambitious, transformational undertakings that have a long-term influence on communities, economies, and future generations.

These initiatives go beyond standard real estate development by addressing social, environmental, and cultural concerns while also contributing to the long-term viability and vibrancy of cities and regions. Legacy initiatives include the following characteristics:

Visionary Leadership: Legacy initiatives are led by visionary leaders who are passionate about making a good change in the world. These leaders motivate stakeholders, organize resources, and gather support for daring projects that challenge the status quo and push the limits of innovation and creativity.

Community participation: Legacy projects need considerable community participation and stakeholder cooperation to ensure that the project meets the needs, values, and ambitions of the local community. Developers communicate with people, companies, government agencies, and nonprofit groups to obtain feedback, resolve issues, and reach an agreement on the project's aims and objectives.

Legacy projects promote sustainability and resilience to reduce environmental impact, protect natural resources, and improve the quality of life for current and future generations. These projects use green construction techniques, renewable energy technology, and resilient design elements to create healthy, lively, and resilient communities.

Cultural Enrichment: Legacy projects honor cultural variety, tradition, and identity by embracing arts, culture, and public places that foster social interaction, creativity, and expression. These initiatives celebrate the community's distinctive character and history, instilling a feeling of belonging and pride in both inhabitants and tourists.

Economic Development: Legacy initiatives promote economic growth and prosperity by providing employment, attracting investment, and rebuilding communities. They drive development in surrounding communities, promote tourism and hospitality, and produce cash streams that benefit local companies, services, and infrastructure.

Examples of noteworthy legacy projects are:

The High Line (New York City): Built on a disused elevated railway track, the High Line is an urban park and greenway that has converted a desolate industrial area into a bustling public place. The initiative has fueled economic growth, increased real estate investment, and served as an example of adaptive reuse and sustainable urban planning.

Masdar City (Abu Dhabi): is a sustainable urban development that aspires to be one of the world's most sustainable cities, with zero carbon emissions and zero trash generation. The project combines renewable energy, water conservation, and smart technology to provide a paradigm for sustainable living and urban design.

REITs and real estate syndications

Real Estate Investment Trusts (REITs) and Real Estate Syndications are two prominent investment structures that enable people to invest in real estate without actually owning the property. Both REITs and syndications provide passive income, portfolio diversification, and real estate exposure. In this complete study, we will look at the fundamentals, structure, advantages, and considerations for REITs and real estate syndications.

Real estate investment trusts (REITs)

A Real Estate Investment Trust (REIT) is a publicly listed firm that owns, manages, or funds income-producing real estate properties. Congress established REITs in 1960 to allow ordinary investors to reap the advantages of owning real estate without the difficulties of direct property ownership. Here are the main features of REITs:

Tax Structure: To be classified as a REIT, a corporation must fulfill specific standards set by the Internal Revenue Service (IRS). REITs are supposed to distribute at least 90% of their taxable revenue to shareholders as dividends, allowing them to avoid paying corporate income taxes at the entity level. Shareholders' dividends from REITs are taxed as regular income.

Liquidity: REITs are traded on major stock exchanges, allowing investors to acquire and sell shares with ease. Unlike direct real estate investments, which may be illiquid and time-consuming to sell, REIT shares can be purchased and sold easily via brokerage accounts.

Diversification: Investing in REITs provides investors with exposure to a diverse portfolio of real estate assets spanning many geographic areas and property kinds. This diversification reduces risks connected with specific properties or markets while increasing overall portfolio stability.

Dividend Income: One of the most appealing aspects of REITs is their potential to provide consistent income in the form of dividends. REITs are legally compelled to transfer a considerable percentage of their taxable revenue to shareholders, making them appealing income-generating assets for yield-seeking investors, retirees, and income-focused portfolios.

Capital Appreciation: In addition to dividend income, REITs can increase capital via property appreciation, rental revenue growth, and strategic value-added activities. Over time, well-managed REITs may provide competitive total returns that surpass conventional fixed-income investments and inflation.

Types of REITs

Equity REITs: Equity REITs invest in and hold income-generating assets including office buildings, retail malls, residential complexes, and industrial facilities. They make money mostly from rental income and property appreciation.
Equity REITs are the most frequent kind of REIT, offering investors exposure to tangible real estate assets.

Mortgage REITs (mREITs): Mortgage REITs (mREITs) buy and hold mortgage-backed securities and other real estate-related debt instruments rather than actual assets. Their primary source of revenue is interest income from mortgage loans and mortgage-backed securities. Mortgage REITs may also use leverage to increase profits, but they are more vulnerable to fluctuations in interest rates and credit risk.

Hybrid REITs: Hybrid REITs are real estate investment trusts that invest in both real estate and mortgage loans, combining characteristics of equity and mortgage REITs. They aim to strike a balance between rental property income and mortgage loan interest income, giving investors diverse exposure to real estate assets and debt instruments.

Real Estate Syndication

Real estate syndication is the process of pooling cash from several investors to participate in real estate projects or assets.

Syndications are often formed as limited partnerships or limited liability companies (LLCs), with one or more sponsors or general partners in charge of finding, purchasing, and administering the investment.

Here are the main features of real estate syndications:

Passive Investing: Real estate syndications provide passive investing alternatives for those who wish to engage in real estate but do not have the time, skills, or resources to do so directly. Passive investors engage funds in the syndicate and earn passive income distributions and possible profits without actively participating in day-to-day activities.

Risk Sharing: Syndications enable investors to distribute the risks and benefits associated with real estate investments across a group of investors. Syndications aim to reduce individual investment risks while increasing total portfolio risk-adjusted returns by pooling resources and diversifying assets.

Access to Deals: Syndications give access to investment possibilities that might otherwise be inaccessible to individual investors owing to high capital requirements, market obstacles, or a lack of deal flow. Syndicators or sponsors use their networks, knowledge, and deal-sourcing ability to uncover promising investment opportunities and negotiate advantageous terms on investors' behalf.

Professional Management: Syndicators or sponsors are responsible for managing syndicated investments, which include property acquisition, due diligence, financing, asset management, and investor communications. They are in charge of carrying out the business strategy, enhancing property performance, and maximizing investor returns all while complying with fiduciary obligations and regulatory constraints.

Profit Sharing: Syndicated investments are often structured such that investors and sponsors share profits and cash flow distributions. Profit-sharing schemes differ based on the investment structure, project type, and sponsor conditions, but they typically emphasize investors' interests and match incentives between investors and sponsors.

Exit Strategies: Syndicators establish distinct exit strategies for syndicated investments, delineating the timeline and criteria for asset disposition or liquidity events. Common exit strategies include property sale, refinancing, or distribution of proceeds to investors upon project completion or maturity. Exit strategies seek to optimize returns for investors and provide liquidity options at various phases of the investment lifecycle.

Final Thoughts

As we come to the end of our journey through "Building Generational Wealth with Real Estate," it's important to reflect on the invaluable lessons, insights, and wisdom gained along the way. Throughout this book, we've explored the transformative power of real estate investing as a vehicle for building and preserving wealth across multiple generations. From understanding the fundamentals of real estate investing to implementing advanced wealth preservation strategies, we've covered a wealth of knowledge designed to empower you on your path to financial prosperity.

Here are some final thoughts to consider as you continue your real estate investing endeavors:

Vision and Purpose: Define your vision for generational wealth and clarify your purpose for investing in real estate. What are your long-term goals and aspirations? How do you envision your wealth impacting future generations? By aligning your investments with your values and goals, you can create a meaningful legacy that transcends financial wealth alone.

Education and Growth: Commit to lifelong learning and continuous growth as an investor. The world of real estate investing is constantly evolving, and staying informed and adaptable is key to long-term success. Take advantage of educational resources, networking opportunities, and mentorship programs to expand your knowledge and refine your skills as an investor.

Risk Management and Resilience: Recognize that real estate investing, like any investment endeavor, comes with inherent risks and uncertainties. While it's important to be proactive in mitigating risks and safeguarding your investments, it's equally important to cultivate resilience and adaptability in the face of challenges and setbacks. Embrace failure as an opportunity for learning and growth, and remain steadfast in your commitment to your long-term vision.

Legacy and Impact: Consider the broader impact of your investments beyond financial returns. How can your real estate endeavors contribute to the betterment of your community, society, and the world at large? Whether through sustainable development practices, community engagement initiatives, or philanthropic endeavors, strive to leave a positive and lasting impact that transcends monetary wealth.

As you embark on this exciting and rewarding journey of building generational wealth with real estate, may you be guided by wisdom, inspired by possibility, and empowered to make a lasting impact for generations to come. Remember that the true measure of wealth lies not in the size of your bank account or the number of properties you own, but in the lives you touch, the legacies you leave, and the difference you make in the world. Here's to your continued success and fulfillment on the path to generational wealth!

Bibliography

Pivar, W. "The Real Estate Developer's Handbook: How to Set Up, Operate, and Manage a Financially Successful Real Estate Development." Atlantic Publishing Company, 2016.

Ben-Eli, D. "Investing in Real Estate: How to Do It Right." New Society Publishers, 2020.

Elder, B. "Multi-Generational Housing in the Urban Context: Beyond Density." Routledge, 2018.

Lee, H., and Brand, J. "Multigenerational Families in Urban Settings: A Guide for Urban Planners and Developers." Palgrave Macmillan, 2017.

Haughwout, P. "Legacy Development: A Practical Guide for Family Wealth Transition." Cognella Academic Publishing, 2020.

Casal, C., and Le Grand, J. "Family Wealth Continuity: Building a Foundation for the Future." John Wiley & Sons, 2016.

Reitman, R. "Real Estate Investment Trusts Handbook." John Wiley & Sons, 2017.

Litzenberger, R. "Real Estate Syndication." Springer, 2018.

www.ingramcontent.com/pod-product-compliance
Lightning Source LLC
Chambersburg PA
CBHW050112230526
45470CB00004B/1796